# Much Ado About Somethings

## Poetry of Life

By Marvin Ginsburg M.D.

# Dedication

This work is dedicated to my life long friend, Skippy Geller who I have known since the third grade in grammar school

Larry Pleet M.D. my best friend for fifty years now gone but always remembered fondly

and
Jack Walker also my very best friend throughout my career

# Acknowledgement

I am extremely grateful to Grace Carras for her help, advice and technical expertise in this work.


I want to express my gratitude to Jasmin and Ian McCarter for their cover artistic creations.

# Table of Contents

Poetic Justice

I can't draw and I can't paint

I haven't the patience of a saint

but first hear my tale and then decide

If you think that I am justified


When I was only in the first grade

and the teacher taught arts and crafts

my mark on art was hardly made

though I gave the class many laughs


This all occurred in the month of April

the teacher drew things of Easter art

I tried to copy against my will

but I couldn't even begin to start

To draw an egg was easy for me

that's about as far as I could go

but that bunny wasn't my cup of tea

I knew I had now met my foe


She announced after much ado

it must be done by end of school today

or stay after school until you do

until you draw the way I say


the other kids drew the rabbit with ease

and I then knew I had much to fear

staying after school made me weak in the knees

no doubt I'd be here for a year

So I can't draw isn't that absurd

perhaps now the answer will unfold

that in a picture I can put into words

and in a metered verse be told


Now I am so very satisfied

but I still can't draw at this time

color texture and size I can describe

and even make all those words rhyme

# First Puppy

When I was only five years old

I wished for a puppy I could hold

one that I might give a name

that would run to me when called by same


We then lived in Mattapan

where daily off to school I ran

and tried to dream how it would feel

To feed my pup his very first meal


Then one day my wish came true

a lost puppy just wandered through

and I recall shouting with glee

I will now name you my sweet puppy

He slept with me throughout the night
and on the next morn I had a fright
that he might not remain at home
I would then again be so alone

Then after much fear and fret
I sadly went to school, you bet
but in my schoolyard at lunchtime
I thought I saw that pup of mine

I wasn't so sure you can see
cause he only slept one night with me

I never really had him identified and when I
got home I sat and cried


Because he left home and followed me

and then off to school he did flee

I feared so then in my mind

my puppy I would never find


While sad at home later that day

mom said my pup had run away

but he was at my school I said

looking for me just to be fed

I cried and cried and felt so blue

because I loved that puppy true

and now I was again so alone

with no puppy in my home


that's why I have two pups today

just in case one should run away

# I Wonder

What makes the wind blow and blow

and where do all the rivers go?

how does the rain fall from the sky

and who lights the light in the firefly?


Why do frogs croak with a deep sound?

why are all our faces so round?

when do cows know to come into the barn

and what makes a big ball of yarn?


Where does the sun go at night?

why do baby kittens have no sight?

when does each day end and start and why
do we all have a heart?


why does a cow moo

and why are you, you?

how does a bird fly?

where does he go and why?


How does the moon know when and where
to rise

and how does it just hang there in the skies?

where does the sun go when it sets

and why does a dog sniff at food it gets?


Why do cats jump and play

and why do they sleep all day?

why can't I think of more to write?

because its late…so goodnight

# What if ?


What if I had a dream last night and it seemed so real

that all the world was upside down, how weird it would feel

all I had to do was to make a vision from my idea

was to speak the words, What if, and it became crystal clear


What if the sky was not blue but rather a shade of green

how funny it would then look and strange it would seem

What if clouds were not white but instead
colored pink

that would surely be an odd sight and also
funny I think


What if bananas were not yellow anymore
but rather colored blue

I would hate them in my cereal and I'm sure
would you


What if the sun rose in the west and set in
the eastern sky

I wouldn't know the time to rise but boy the
time would fly

What if the front was really the back and up
was really down

I'd be walking on my head and my feet not
on the ground

What if an orange was not orange but
instead the color red

We'd have to call it a red

now get that one in your head


What if all the colors were not anymore the
same

just polka dots and big old stripes wouldn't
that be a shame

What if the zebra had no more stripes

because all the black ones all turned white


What if we faced backwards with our feet
pointing to the rear

I would see where I'd been but not where to
go I fear

What if I continued this thought and my face
pointed in the opposite direction

well I'd never get to where I was going

this I'd better mention

What if left was right and right was left and I
thought that I knew

I would turn to the left that I thought was
right and bump right into you

What if we were all at peace and loved one
another

even if we were of different races and also of
different color

the whole world would be changed and no
more in a rift

now then it would be very worthwhile to think

What if?

# For My Grandson at Christmas
## To Blake

Because you have been a good boy

Santa will leave you an extra toy

from Santa's big house it came

a very long electric train


He will also leave for you to play

what was that he heard you say?

a  toy reindeer pulling the sleigh

for you to play with every day

All this year you have been so great

so Santa on this very date

promises that he will appear

at your house at Christmas next year


so be very good and also kind

and your mama you should mind

then Santa will again bring toys

to all good girls and all good boys

# In Memory of Bruce My Son

It was this time of year in 1972

I just met two boys, Bruce and Shane

Bruce so timid and shy he wouldn't even
play a game

with a spirit as gentle as softly fallen rain


He then grew up and became a young man

and yearned to fulfill the desires of his heart

he, his grandpa and I, off to the recruiters we
ran

it was on that day, I believe he found his start


He enlisted and was sent to Fort Brag

to learn how to repair copters and such

proud he was and we also were glad

that he loved the Army and his work so much


He was assigned to the 82nd Airborne

and jumped in the Panama invasion

then to Riyadh and fought in Desert Storm

to return again home in celebration


Four years excellence in service to his flag

his commanders judged him to be the very best

was decorated with medals on return to Fort Brag

to his character and devotion they all did attest

Like a storm flooding on an unsuspecting tomorrow

that acquiesces silently but just as fast

our  many tears shed to help our sorrow

allowing us to recall memories of the past


Throughout his short life's journey, he tried the course

insisting on standing up all alone

eventually overcome by an unknown force

but at last returned to us at home

# A Son's Tribute to His Parents
## Hand in Hand

Fifty years side by side
Sam the groom, Jean his bride
began their marriage in thirty four
soon thereafter two sons they bore

In nineteen thirty six on leap year's day
again in thirty nine on the seventeenth of
May
one named Marv the other Bob
and their father with barely a job

The hurricane came we were at the ocean
all roads closed during the commotion
dad to the rescue for wife and son
getting us out before any damage done


Times were tough in thirty nine
depression years without a dime
but you both did well succeed
we never wanted for clothes or feed

We moved to Mass. in forty one
so dad might fulfill his obligation
at Hingham Shipyard he did work

while overhead fears of war did lurk


Visiting the Franklin Park Zoo

asking dad if he had gum and candy too

providing for us with his two hands

I remember when I caught fish and he
caught cans


Our childhood I remember well

the love and comfort and sometimes hell

Bob and I always in a fight

throughout each day and every night


Causing perhaps some  real embarrassment

like the days you had to scrape up the rent

but throughout it all and despite the threats

my life with you leaves no regrets


I always felt loved even when I was bad

which was more than many kids had

your understanding and direction for our growth

nurtured character in us both


In my later life when I was low

with life's problems and events unfair

It felt so good to really know

In you both we had more than our share

Your anniversary and mom's birthday come
close together

in you both there is no inclement weather

so with my love, please accept this trip

upon the ocean on the Sitmar ship


This is but a token of what you deserve

that I can't ever repay

all the things you did for us, yesterday and
today

# Here a Kitty, There a Kitty

Some twenty five cats more or less

abound our house and make a mess

but we have no frets  and don't even care

about all those cats and all that hair


They jump and twist and even play

it seems they never stop all the day

Kato Spuds and all the rest

we love them all, they are the best


Kitties here and kitties there, I just don't think
it's right

finding places to hide up high remaining out
of sight

they claw and scratch and  even sometimes
bite

beginning when we retire and throughout the
night


Kitties and cats we've got by the score

I pray to God we acquire no more

their names are hard to memorize

they look alike and so do their eyes


There's Spats so named for markings on his
feet

then there's Mama Kitty who thinks she's so
elite

and Kato not because he's a friend of OJ

then Puka who is always running away

Mr. Spuds sleeps in our bed while lying on
his back

and his brother Spats prefers to be in a
brown paper sack

while Spuds will cuddle upon command

Spatsmeister will try and grab your hand


And sometimes he tackles my leg somehow

insisting that I stop and play right now

his two paws clutch as if to say pay me
some mind

if not I'll do a trick of a different kind


Nada's so aloof and has so much to say

and also in our bed she must lay

where she washes her face and then her
paws

but all her purring drowns out my snores

# Tonsil Trouble

At about the age of nine

I got sore throats all the time

sometimes even an ear infection

did escape the doctor's inspection


After many doses of penicillin

the doctor asked if I was willin

for a new type of sore throat cure

to which I answered yes, I'm sure


So off we went by trolly bus

I never even made a fuss

for what I imagined in my mind

was a medicine of a different kind

I ate not breakfast on that morning
and thought that very strange and annoying
but it never even dawned on me
that there was indeed some secrecy

But soon thereafter as I suspected
that in my throat where that thing nested
needed treatment not with medication
but rather in stead by an operation

and the doctor's cure for me alright
was now directly in his sight
I should have guessed or maybe known

not what he said but by his tone


Then he again examined me

I didn't make a peep

said he, those must come out

and I'd just fall asleep

and when I woke my throat would be sore

but I would never have tonsillitis any more

# A  Father's Influence

He was such a very hard working Man

twas my dad, his name was Sam

short in stature, about five feet two

Not very many people he knew


Just a simple family type

went to work without a gripe

few different jobs over the years

much hardship and as much tears


I remember when I was a young lad

the toys and things I never had

but warm memories of him and I

fishing together under the blue sky


We would arise early on that morn

the sky still black before the dawn

we gathered our tackle and gobbled some
food

all excited and anticipating the mood


Making lunch and stuffing it into a brown
paper sack

into the old Plymouth, I jumped in the back

we tried being quiet so not to awaken
mother

the front seat now grabbed by my brother


Off to the lake to catch the fish

dreaming of the big one and making that
wish

usually getting lost on many a morn

arriving at the lake just after dawn


We drove to that old tackle shop at the creek

buying bait inside that was unique

the fish we were after needed their favorite
food

also the lures that were certain to set their
mood


Inside I recall the smell of the brine

And the little old man wrinkled with time

A cigarette in his mouth with wisps of smoke

And a rasping cough whenever he spoke

Some small talk about what's biting today

we bought the lures that worked yesterday

this was the best bait and the lures to use

The bait man swore we could hardly lose


We rented an old row-boat, I remember was
green

it looked to me it was leaking at the seam

dad and I took turns at rowing to that special
spot

anchoring at Lilly pads we thought would be
hot


Mist rising from the serene surface water

thinking this was the spot we oughta

the balmy summer breeze from the west
we casted our rods and hoped for the best


What a thrill when I got my first bite
I jumped around and shouted with delight
my rod bending right over the side
shouting a two pounder,  but I really lied


Dad fussed and fidgeted to keep the boat
steady
not saying much till he was ready
that's one day I will never forget
whoever catches the most wins the bet

Extreme huger struck at about eleven
the last snack I had was at seven
so I grabbed for that brown paper bag
before my strength would surely lag

On the way home dad would often say
I'm so tired I'll probably lose the way
I sure wish you were old enough to drive
we probably won't get home till after five

Now whenever I think of those days
I find it's fishing that I crave
but perhaps it's not really the fish I enjoy
but rather when he was my dad and I was
his boy

When I am fishing now or only thinking of it
I sense his love even more I will admit
and as those days flash into my mind
I remember him as gentle and kind


If I can only but accomplish the same
with my two sons Mark and Shane
showing love, concern and being their friend
then they'll feel the same about me in the
end


So if it's fishing we can share together
we will go often no matter the weather
not only just to catch fish but also to talk

Just to be together and go for a walk

for there's much more to life than I can ever say

It's loving your sons together in that very special way

# The Election

In nineteen hundred and ninety, when the election was completed

the Republicans all looked around and saw they were defeated

now Bill and Hillary were in the house of white and tried so hard to lead

but to their dismay the populace did not their politics heed


Health care was the first lady's passion and pursued it without direction

for hers was not an elected office although without detection

summoning her friends and, calling for a meeting

nothing became of it despite her leading

Came Paula on the scene claiming to be
molested

and the Whitewater cronies some already
arrested

the final tax hike took place despite
objections from the

other party

Democrats congratulated one another
feeling hail and hearty

They felt very good for it was the people they
protected

not the slightest clue that liberals were soon
to be ejected

these liberals say, let government do for you
and be your sugar dad

and despite what just happened they are still
so very mad


Pointing to California and to prop 187 they
feel pompous in the senate

for it did matter much what people said even
if from Kemp and Bennet

there are some who would be angry at the
stand these men stated

but others who simply think that they should
be hated

that's not here or there as it was never from
a minion

It really only stemmed from two men's
opinion

Now Bill and Hillary can shout and scream

and try to fulfill their liberal dream

it won't happen again in ninety five or six

and Bill won't be the donkey's pick


For the people are now too smart you know

to give the democrats another go

so let's all sit and relax

just watch congress drop the tax


Led by the solid ones with soul who have the
people's wish at heart

deliver their contracts promised at the pole
right from the very start

Congressman Foley, from Washington if you
please

he did indeed feel the squeeze

from his electorate that said no to him

and to the rest of his political kin


All the republicans who ran succeeded

all the voters did what was needed

to eject the cronies all liberals to a T

so you just wait till ninety-six Bill and Hillary

# Horsing Around

Out early in the morn with coffee in the cup

what fun bestows us, let's giddy on up

all gathered together as though at a
convention

the wacky and weirdos all with one intention


To ride and race through all types of terrain

looking back to see distance you've gained

running amok and running amiss

is there no sport as easy as this?


When you are beat and have run many a mile

and pull up at the vet stop with a smile

to hay your horse and water him with care

cooling him down quickly, if you dare


He better not shiver or his temp won't drop

and the vet will say you have to stop

to continue the race but you're late out of the
check

you ride like crazy to catch up but what the
heck


By the time you do and are in the lead

the finish line is what you really need

because your butt is tired and your bones
are sore

that's not stopping you for doing more

Check his pulse and then respiration

now you feel all that desperation

because your horse is lame and it was your
mission

to win that coveted Best Condition


You shouldn't worry and you shouldn't fret

for you'll race again, I will bet

for the fun of staying awake all night long

and the excitement of the race, that old song


To win to win above all else I must

and in this old nag I must surely trust

to get me over these mountain trails

and over the snow and through the gales

So you can return to camp and say

you can't wait to do it again someday

probably in only a week or two

If you find your horse's shoe


Then put it back on in a proper manner

so it won't come off in a canter

check if you can now use a bit

and then on a soft saddle sit


To ride in and out of those Vet checks with
ease

would most certainly your ego please

for it would demonstrate beyond a doubt

that your horse and you had the clout

You would then go hell bent for leather

no matter what, no matter the weather

because you do what you do best

that's to run the race and test the test

# Memories and Advice to My Dearest Friend

Larry is my good friend

I believe he'll do it in the end

he'll invent that unique machinery

and get rich, you just wait and see


Something great is his intention

to develop a process or an invention

this is really not any kind of joke

but better happen now so he won't go broke


He works so hard at all he does

on his inventions he gets a buzz

and he is also a great physician

but medicine is not he's wishin'

Rather then to hit that jackpot
to become rich now and a lot
that he might retire in great style
and help his friends all the while

To buy that pacific isle retreat
is something to ponder really neat
but it's right now you've got to live
and to the IRS you must still give
a part of your life's blood each day
which is equal to six months pay

Medicine is no longer any fun

and from it we have to run

for we've managed here and also there

but we are not moving anywhere


We lost our income that's for sure

yet we still must treat and cure

all those patients who bitch and moan

while we scurry to the bank to make a loan


So please my friend go sell your knowledge

no need  for you to return to college

whatever your ideas or what you make

please sell your house on the lake

Phyllis I fear does hate that place

and is rapidly tiring of the rat race

so make it happen and grab the money

Then  go have fun with your honey

# Tolerating Your Wife's Preparations for Thanksgiving

Turkey, potatoes, veggies and cake

cook, peel, pare and bake

more than twenty four hours in the day

that's it wifey, that's the way


Mop, shop, stop and slop

spread that frosting on the top

on your newest culinary creation

which no doubt will be a sensation


Horses, cats and dogs to feed

all this do you really need?

about all this, I will indeed complain

you say you love it but what a pain

There is no question but what I see

needs alteration with sobriety

tension, anxiety with a loud noise

coming from the stove as you poise

Moan, groan, scream and bitch

wait a while and hear my pitch

cause next year you'll be seeing

we're kicking back on the Caribbean

Or perhaps on another island terrific

no question I'll choose the South Pacific

Hawaii, Kona or maybe Kawaii
just relax and I'll tell you why


You're too tired and also spastic
but you are  definitely so fantastic
in all you do and all you prepare
I'm here to tell you, I really do care


Will you with all this, cease and desist
knock it off if you get my gist
for you make me tired and you make me sad
seeing you frazzled makes me so mad

You say you do and you say you don't
you say you will and you say you won't
stop the work and forget the pie
come to the beach and with me lie

In the sun and play in the surf
that will surely be a better turf
then stressing out this holiday
let's celebrate it another way

I love you and you love me
so together let us both flee
from all this and all that strain
we're out of here next year, it's insane!!

# The Picture

I awaken to summer winds caressing the
trees

the western sky a shimmering blue

sun illuminating silver trim to Aspen leaves

while early morning light peeked through


I hear the mountain jay's scream in a nearby
tree

scolding and shrieking at a bird of prey

and the rat a tat tat of the woodpecker's
song

drumming its march and continuing it's play

In the forest dimly lit at first morn's light

the dogs so excited as we struck the way

and the trampled trail covered with leaves

this will indeed be a great day


Then ahead in the deep grassy meadow

stands a doe with her spotted fawn

a quiet scene of beauty and serenity

on this early warm summer morn


I had no camera to capture the sight

and I thought that was too bad

this scene would surely be lost all right

a permanent memory was not to be had

But why not make my eyes the camera

and record this sight forever

then when I want to see it again

all I need do is to remember


What a novel idea, my brain has film in color

recording all events that the eye sees

film ages in years and loses it's luster

But I can record it myself with ease


I can look at the world as a book

no light or shadows to ever worry about

not even giving focus a look

the picture will be perfect, that's never in
doubt

In the future, when that scene ,I should wish

and can't recall where the picture was shot

I conjure it up like a satellite dish

and marvel at the picture I got

## A Penny Saved

Oh Shane my boy, Shane my son
on your own a job to be done
do it your way with individuality
I shall be impressed can't you see

A long hard way you have come
and when it's all said and done
it  pleases me to no end
now this short poem I will send

Because you may not even know
that I really love you so

this sage advice I want to say

your money must be put away


A little cash every time you're paid

and then of you it will be said

Shane bought it with money he sequestered

even though he felt so pestered


Growing so by the nth degree

and by then you will surely see

that though the advice was free

you have saved enough money


To buy a house or maybe a car

even to travel near and far

then to admit to save was fun

when it's in the bank, it's all done


You'll then have cash to spend; be glad

or perhaps send it back to dad

maybe just let it grow in the bank

and one day soon, me , you'll thank


For cash is king, surely you note

it comes not easy but will by rote

tuck it away by repetition

let that always be your mission

# Kindergarten Fears

The first day of kindergarten I stood by the
door

I cried and cried and didn't want to stay

because I was sure I'd go home no more

while the kids inside beckoned me to play


But they were kids and some were bad

still others made me feel so sad

then I saw colored crayons on each table

it was this sight that mede me able


I remember all we learned to do that day

to draw with crayons and to mold with clay.

after an hour we snacked on crackers and
drinks

I was so scared I knew not what to think


Then I learned how to cut and paste

and to create kids stuff with such haste

then we all sat and we all sang a song

Except me, I sang words all wrong


I heard the school bell ring we all left the
room in single file

there stood my mother with a smile

said she, "I never left you at all

but was here waiting in the hall"

Had I known then I wouldn't have cried

on that first day when I tried

so hard to be brave and not feel forlorn

because I really thought my mom had gone


Returning thereafter was always a delight

since I had now experienced the light

and now I had conquered the fear of being
alone

because when the bell rang, I could then go
home

# Nature's Fight for Superiority
## The Wind and the Tree

Oh I think that a tree must certainly be

an example given by God of course

and so I've noticed  when I see

that the wind blows with violent force


Like when it bellows through the tree

and accelerates so the leaves hear it

it seems to say you shall bow down to me

else I shall break your spirit


Wind is the fury of all the storms

or it may vanish or may pretend

then once again reappear in other forms

harboring much greater devastation to send


It desires that the tree shake and tremble

raising it's pitch with great urgency

commanding that the tree now bow down

if not then to suffer its atrocity


The tree to this demand sustains not flexion

for the more violent the raging wind blew

their limbs arched further in the opposite
direction

not doing at all what they were ordered to do

Then the storm ebbs and the tree stands tall

Looking like they always were forever

I'm joyous that they have never met their fall

though tried by the wind's  failed endeavor


But the wind loses it's temper again and
again

trying to extract a genuflect

still haven't learned what we as men

come to know as a mutual respect


And if the tree has fallen to earth

it's seeds have been blown from the site

so many new trees will will then give birth

on one day soon to continue the fight

# Winter Comfort

It's really funny when you see a sight

your mind begins to wander

as though you're high upon a kite

and through past years you saunter


That nip on your face at the end of
December

creating those childhood visions so clear

growing up in the East and what I remember

are ever in my mind and so crystal clear


Blue skies with clouds aligned in rows

mountains covered in mounds of white

the western sun in finality glows

producing umbrage to all in sight


The chill of night making it's indolent way

fusion with stars hanging in the sky

clues me of that long ago day

living in the bleak winter of R.I.


An old oil stove with fire lapping at its door

was the source of our comfort at night

many days we'd shovel snow till we could no
more

returning home to welcome that warm sight


We loved those snowstorms when the snow
piled high

which meant we could work for pay

brother Bob, my friends and I

shoveled walks, paths and an occasional
driveway


When a winter storm hit hard, schools had to
close

early morn we listened to the radio for
confirmation

calling each other to announce the roads

all impassable and we shouted with such
elation


We shoveled for an hour or a half at each job

fifty cents or a dollar was the average fee

dividing the cash half for me and half for Bob

customers so delighted, they even paid more
you see.


As the day grew longer the sun in the west
set

now we felt hungry tired and cold

we still kept working although soaking wet

Returning home for a pot of gold


Not really that precious metal, please
understand

because here we felt love, warmth and
protection

chicken soup I thought the best in the land

though we never had much of a selection

Now I sit and think about moving to the cold

I shiver at the thought of shoveling the white
stuff

for in the warm weather I'd rather grow old

of snow shovels and freezing I've had
enough


But the true reason for this negative reaction

can easily be noted,  if you desire

for I could never again have that satisfaction

of eating chicken soup by the old stove's fire

# Attempting to Please Your Wife

## AKA

## The Fencemeisters

There stands a house in Colorado way on up
high

that needed many fences to be built

my wife asked my friend the old tennis pro
and I

we stared at each other without any guilt


For who else could ever even attempt this
task

to sink post holes in a straight line

who could possibly place the holes, I asked

and to do it all in a record time

Said Ed to me and I did agree

let's get going on this simple task

jumping into the truck turning the key

to our chagrin we were out of gas


Well after a while, close to an hour just
talking

we loaded the truck with all our gear

cometh my wife angry and daunting

we were on our third can of beer


You haven't even dug any of the holes

she said in a soft voice so demure

you also forgot to bring along the poles

you've never done this before I'm sure


Now Marty, said Ed to her with glee

we've certainly put up many a fence

give us a few hours then you'll see

Marv and I have much say and sense


She let us be and we laughed and joked

because we  really never had done this task
before

then cometh the storm and we both got
soaked

so we ran all the way home in that  heavy
downpour


Well did you do what I asked you to do?

she said with such inquisitive candor

I looked at Ed who she was talking to

and quickly outside I did meander


Now see here Marty said Ed with a straight
face

your husband was the cause of this mess

we never even put one pole in place

drank too much beer, we had to rest


So the next day early in the morn

we again tried to put up the fence

between taking a nap or eating lunch, we
were torn

we decided to do both that made good
sense

Now another day just bit the dust

and we accomplished nothing at all

Marty said we failed her trust

and many nice names she did us call


Ed and I really attempted for a week

to dig at least one more hole in the ground

Marty then came back to take another peek

with a thundering  shriek making a deafening
sound


Said I it was Ed who changed the height

the rails were now uneven and not so
straight

the fence had become  such a miserable
sight

and now it was getting really late


So we left for the house, since its was now
so late

and we were famished from all our work

we weren't even paid the minimum hourly
rate

and to boot the old pro was such a jerk


We thought we'd finish it for it was so clear

and Ed told Marty we should make a plan

why not wait and do it all next year

then we hauled our butts out and ran

# To My Daughter at Christmas

When you were such a little tyke

you wished that Santa bring a bike

or a dress or maybe a baby doll

so we then meandered through the mall


You grew older and also wise

giving me so many ties

then to your dad you did query

why all the people were so merry


For when you were so very young

and Christmas songs were happily sung

you wished you could,  you wished you might

have your wish become real that very night


I was Santa then for your dream

and it did to me really see

that when I bought for you that gift

not to open till the twenty fifth


I remember the excitement in your eyes

tearing open gifts and undoing the ties

today I hope seeing you the same again

for you to be as happy now as you were so
then


Inside this is something you will like, I think

it could be blue or possibly pink

I hope you enjoy it and it makes you happy

but if not, please don't tell your pappy

# Winter in Rhode Island

The silence of green wherever I gaze

coupled with the failure of leaves to fall

Reminds me of the years so long ago

the way winter taking it's exact toll


It's not very cold in old Cali

the winds never howl or blow

I feel quite deprived and cheated

here out west we could use some snow


I still recall that biting wind

The flurry dancing round my head

that stinging fury of the snow

Bit my face till it felt dead

I rise from my bed, and the floor feels like ice
the furnace died sometime last night
Someone must have forgot to shovel the
coal!
I rush to the cellar to correct this plight

Turn the key, pump the gas, it still won't run
it's too, cold and the oil too thick inside
blowing my warm breath on my frozen
thumb
I keep turning the key to my frozen ride.

I can't drive anyhow, the snow's so slick
hanging like pie crust over the whole car

I have to get to the bus stop pretty darn
quick

school is starting soon, and I must walk far.


The bitter wind cutting through my clothes

I cannot hide from it's heinous act

I trudge on the street as it goes

then suddenly the chill leaves my back


Overhead the skies are dull and gray

day after day they loom above threatening to
hold

no sun for more than a week, I can say

and morning after morning my fingers stay
frozen cold

My face is red, stinging and very wet

I slip and fall often in the deep white stuff

cold snow soaking through my pants and yet

through ice-cold pants and feet, I'm still
tough


I dream of hot coffee each morning;

when I need to get warm, it's the most
reliable tool.

Now hunger strikes, and makes me weak;

I decide, "there's no way I'm going to
school!"


It's eight-thirty, and I'm already running late!

So why not just hit the movies at noon?

A pie or a muffin also sounds great,

so I'll head to the coffee shop soon.


After the movies, I returned to school

just in time for indoor track.

All of my friends obeyed an unspoken rule;

if I didn't show up, they'd jump my back.


Then home with my friend in his '39 Ford,

the door half-gone and the window stuck
down.

On top of it all, the heater is broken,

but it won't stop us from cruising the town.


I slouched down in front of the teachers we
passed

so no one could see my face at all,

for fear they might recall I wasn't in class

and then decide to give my mother a call!

# Impressions

Just sauntering where the waters chase

those footprints no longer remain

one flush of the sea in such great haste

regarding the prints in utter disdain


What was copied to the sand is now gone

and the obliging sea reveals powerful surges

toying with the beach though it were a pawn

then moving the sand wherever it urges


It has naught to do all day in the sun

but lap the shore and remove all trace

for where many have chosen there to run

can never be proven at all in this case


Why do the waves forever clean

the beach and remove all physical evidence

I think I know the answer and it does seem

to make a lot of common sense


The sand is a permanent history of things of
the past

as it records everyone who has ever walked
upon it

but it must be wiped clean and done very
fast

or there would be no more place for the
record to fit

# Bora Bora Beautiful

Ripples of water lapping at the soft white
sand

Irregular mountain peaks jutting straight from
the sea

a pallet of splendorous colors that go hand
in hand

but changes as the sun strikes the land
intensely


Bora Bora always the same in January or
June

is only a spec of this great French Polynesia

I fear the days will pass so quick and too
soon

and I will have to leave this insatiable leisure

Shades of clouds, piled one upon another

they line up atop of each mountain peak

summoned to muster by winds that hover

seeming to have a defined purpose to seek




White billows first followed by those shaded
gray

removing from all vision in the sky so blue

some move on throughout the heat of the
day

others remain dauntless in order to cool

The sky is full of clouds that can hold water
no more

to give life to every tree, plant and vine

the somber dry ones cry tears upon the
shore

the sky so bleak as though the sun shall
never shine


The water dressed in aqua, blue and hues of
green

she walked along leaving her footprints
within waters reach

this place must surely be an illusion, it really
did seem

but there was nothing left to show she had
ever walked on this beach

# Bora Bora Storm Undecided

Rat a tat tat the raindrops play

early in the morn while in bed you lay

awakened you are by that rapid drum beat

open the door and you don't feel the heat


Boats on the water and the catamaran is
gone

divers being ferried on this gray morn

and all these people run and scuttle about

but if you don't speak French you have no
clout


The regal slender palms standing so tall

others acutely bent as though to fall

but more rising straight arrow to the sky

under their palm leaves do coconuts lie




Then as fast as that rainstorm started

the skies lightened and the clouds then
parted

and in a moment the sun broke right through

maybe a warm beach and swimming for you



This now signaled the end of the storm

and raised the temperature from luke to
warm

air remained dense and so very wet

I think this is not quite so over just yet


The day stays balmy and the soft wind blows

no sun is yet present and the clouds are in
rows

the moisture in the air is so easily seen

and the menacing sky looks evil and mean


The horizon now can't easily be discerned

calm water changes to green and is churned

those ominous clouds hover at the sea's
surface

so quickly as if done with definite purpose


Overhead the blues suddenly turn too gray

as though it was trying hard to convey

wind now increasing a few knots in speed

another tropical storm is not far, take heed!

# A Wife's Shopping for a Bora Bora Pareo

We were awakened very early at four AM
before dawn

by the song and dance of the rain upon the
roof

With a mounting crescendo all through the
morn

lakes of water all around offered up their
proof


The large umbrellas opened on high

they all scurry to breakfast on pavement wet

while rivers of water floated on by

we won't see sun this day,  you can bet

So off on the town bus to of course just
browse

my lovely wife must find that certain thing

we found every boutique that sanity allows

then I began that favorite song to sing


Let's go let's go here comes the bus

we better move fast to avoid the fuss

my watch tells me its time for this bus ride

I looked at my love, she knew that I had lied


Now she won't really care,  if I get my way

only one more place she just had to go

I've still got money for many a day

and no doubt she will find another Pareo

# Turtle Island Fiji

The water shades of blue-green

the beach is white

puffy clouds loom in the distance

day relinquishes to returning shadows of
night

the sun simmers the sea with indifference


The horizon seems to meld clouds to the
ocean

boats all day lie apathetic in this lagoon

birds have all stopped their sweet songs
and motion

Remaining so still with the rising moon

Rain plummets down beating flowers and
grass

pools of water collected under all the trees

sky holding gray suggesting more to amass

with no more evidence of wind or angry seas


The tempest suddenly appears to die

a few scattered leaves, a direct indication

the sun never even tried to rise

remaining obscure in righteous indignation


Tomorrow will bring a different play

clouds will be gone and remain aloof

just another balmy tropical day

sunshine all day revealing the proof

# The Windsurfer

What wondrous colors in this blue lagoon

emanating not only from the ocean by itself

the surfers sail played to the winds tempest
tune

struggling to avoid the approaching coral
shelf


Hop right on and grab the boom

then steer trying hard to keep balance while
the board rolls

the wind changes direction but you've
naught to fear

as

you are becoming one of those brave souls

Just stand up straight and remain at the
ready

as the wind drops and becomes still and
quiet

try to tack and change your position, now
steady

it must be great fun if you  really buy it


Fall over one side and then to the other

trying to find gravity's center of the board

on the beach soaking the rays I'd rather

I, my dear am not out of my gourd

I have just realized at the end of the day

you are being towed by a boat to the shore

what an adventure on this wind surfer's bay

surely your body and bones must be sore


It appears something is lacking in what
you've learned

what goes to sea must always return to the
sand

not skimming over the waves with a body so
burned

but powered by the wind not by a boat
lending a hand

# The Eternal Play

Enter stage left with the wind moving the
birch leaves in the opposite direction

and from the right, the sun, through the
clouds with a bright shine

then falls a rain drop to the water and
destroys the unblemished reflection

the lake reacts to the disturbance to the rain
in response to this sign


The stage master has cast the signal that
calls forth the light

the water and land change from black to the
colors in the artist's brush

I await the play to begin in the midst of the
amazing sight

each part of the creation has a piece to play
and brings forth it's special touch


The lake at midnight follows with the
shimmer of green in demonstration

each of the tree branches and leaves alter
color in but a minute

tone intensity on the land directed by the
sun's orchestration

we view nature about as it speaks

it's lines with moving spirit in it


I watch from the audience in silence as
excitement abounds at the opening moment

remaining ignorant and unaware of the great
story and even the lines

again the same players who are cast daily
are all now present

among them are the sun, moon, stars, rivers,
winds and the pines


Rehearsals never need happen and are not a
must for the endless cast

their parts all played with grandiosity ad lib
and exactly on cue

the scene moves moment to moment and is
no more a task

then the change of the heavens from black,
amber, orange or blue


The first  wind is so warming gentle and the
waters are not stirred

not a ripple or any imperfection can be seen
on the glass like surface

dawn then breaks with the peeping of the
sun, not a sound to be heard

the actors all standing silently in the wings
each with a defined purpose


Then over and over each and every day as
long as we live

we are so privileged to witness the play,  but
always with the lines rewritten

there is need for a new twist each of the
actors must create and give

the wonder of it all,  that each day is so
different

leaves me so truly smitten

# THE END

www.ingramcontent.com/pod-product-compliance
Lightning Source LLC
Chambersburg PA
CBHW080716120726
48001CB00010B/3042